NEVE

The Walter D. Strong Family
1900 - 1978 & Beyond

With 50 snapshots from the
Strong family photo collection

Outskirts Press, Inc.
Denver, Colorado

For information:
Jean Strong
1478 Niagara Street
Springdale, Arkansas 72762
Email: BJStrong25@aol.com

The opinions expressed in this manuscript are solely the opinions of the authors and do not represent the opinions or thoughts of the publisher. The copyright owner represents and warrants that she either owns or has the legal right to publish all material in this book.

Never Say Never, The Walter B. Strong Family,
1900-1978 & Beyond
All Rights Reserved.

Copyright © 2008 Jean Strong
V1.0

COVER PHOTO:
Thelma Strong rides a mule named Ida into
the Grand Canyon in 1956. Photo by daughter.

This book may not be reproduced, transmitted, or stored in whole or in part by any means, including graphic, electronic, or mechanical without the express written consent of the copyright owner or the publisher except in the case of brief quotations embodied in critical articles and reviews.

Outskirts Press, Inc.
http://www.outskirtspress.com

ISBN: 978-1-4327-1044-6

Outskirts Press and the "OP" logo are trademarks belonging
to Outskirts Press, Inc.

PRINTED IN THE UNITED STATES OF AMERICA

The Walter Strong Family

1951. Eileen Minor, Ruth, Maurice Minor, Thelma, Doris, Jean, George, and Walter B. Strong.

Strong Family Tree

Linn County, Iowa
Note: m = married; (0) = # children

Luman Mastin Strong (1803-1867)
m1 Nancy Griswold (7 children)

↓

Henry G. Strong (1834-1915)
m Christina Lutz (4)

↓

George Albert Strong (1870-1936)
m1 Nettie L. Bowman (2) m2 Ida M. Crowley (0)

↓

Walter Benjamin Strong (1901-1951)
m **Thelma** Iris Oliver (1900-1978) (6)

↓

Eileen (4)	Jean	George (2)	Doris (4)	Ruth (1)
Maurice	(single)	Darlene	Norman	Stan Mazgay (1)
Minor		Moser	Neal	John Armstrong
↓		↓	↓	↓

Oliver Family Tree

Maryland, North Carolina, Indiana, Iowa
Note: m = married; (0) = # children

John Oliver (c1699-1741)
m Margaret _____
↓

George Oliver (1726/7-1786)
m1 Jemima Reagan (9)
↓

James Oliver (c1756-1840)
m Susannah Lemons (8)
↓

Samuel Oliver (1794-1843)
m Ruth Obedience Alley (13)
↓

John Hiram Oliver (1831-1920)
m Elizabeth "Eliza" Drennan (11)
↓

Samuel Ellsworth Oliver (1858-1931)
m Mary Elizabeth Morgan (11)
↓

Thelma Iris Oliver (1900-1978)
m October 6, 1921 (6)
Walter B. Strong (1901-1951)
↓

Eileen E. (Mrs. Maurice Minor)
(Betty) Jean Strong
George W. Strong (Darlene Moser)
Doris Mae (Mrs. Norman Neal)
Ruth Ann Mazgay (Mrs. John Armstrong)

About Our Ancestors

GRANDCHILDREN OF WALTER AND THELMA STRONG are of the sixth generation, stemming from the earliest known Strong ancestor—Luman Mastin Strong, born in Orange County, Vermont (1803-1867) and arrived in Iowa via Ohio in 1839. Luman's son, Henry G., (1834-1915) married Christina Lutz (1839-1910), and their son, George A. (1870-1936) married Nettie Bowman. Their son, Walter B. (1901-1951) married Thelma Oliver. As the "grand children" marry and produce children, the family line extends.

On the maternal side, stemming from the earliest known Oliver ancestor, grandchildren are of the ninth generation. Thelma Oliver Strong, who arrived in Iowa in 1915, researched her Olivers in the 1970s by corresponding and sharing information with relatives in Arizona, California, Oklahoma and Indiana.

> ["*Sketches of the Olivers, a Family History, 1726 to 1966*" by Colonel Hugh R. and Margaret T. Oliver, 577 pp., 1987, contains extensive documentation for our early Olivers. The book also includes the interesting history of the Cades Cove, Tennessee Olivers whose property became part of the Great Smoky Mountain National Park. A pilot in WWII and Korea, Col. Oliver descends from the Cades Cove Olivers. The cabin of George Oliver's son, John, is preserved as a point of interest in the park, but the families were bitter about the loss of their land in the 1930s.]

George Oliver and four of his sons fought in the fierce Revolutionary War battle at Guilford Courthouse, a North Carolina hamlet, on March 15, 1781. They came to North Carolina from Maryland and settled along the Dan River.

We trace our Oliver family line from John and Margaret Oliver, in the late 1600s, to George (1756-1786) and Jemima (Reagan) Oliver,

James (1756-1840) and Susannah (Lemons) Oliver, and Samuel (1794-1843) and Ruth Obedience (Alley) Oliver in North Carolina.

After her husband Samuel died, Ruth Obedience Oliver in 1845 moved her family to Indiana. Their son, John Hiram Oliver (1831-1920) married Elizabeth "Eliza" Drennan (both died in California) and their 11 children included Samuel Ellsworth Oliver (1858-1931), father of Thelma Strong.

Samuel Ellsworth Oliver (1858-1931) married Mary Elizabeth Morgan, and their daughter, Thelma (1900-1978) married Walter B. Strong in 1921.

Walter and Thelma Strong and the families of their surviving children are the central subjects of *The Walter B. Strong Family*.
—*J.S.*

1957. Thelma sits atop Acadia Mountain near Bar Harbor, Maine, during a six-week research tour with her daughter for *Life* magazine

Born in 1900 Indianapolis, Thelma Oliver became a teenage bookkeeper in a Cedar Rapids shoe store, married a farmer at 21, bobbed her hair, produced six children, and was widowed at 51. Thelma finished her autobiography in 1977, six months before she died.

Daughter Jean is writing a memoir about her long publishing career in Iowa, New York City, Philadelphia, Washington, D.C. and northwest Arkansas, her current home.

Dedicated to the "Grand Kids" of Walter & Thelma

SIXTH GENERATION

Their Grandchildren (11)

1944	David Minor	Dec. 7
1948	Mark Minor	Sept. 12
1951	Neil Minor	July 31
1953	Allen Strong	March 16
1955	Janice Neal	March 12
1955	Elaine Minor	Dec. 24
1957	Pam Strong	Dec. 12
1958	Joe Armstrong	June 2
1958	Rick Neal	Aug. 4
1961	Steve Neal	March 8
1962	Karen Neal	Oct. 29

SEVENTH GENERATION

Their Great-grandchildren (11)

1976	Leslie Strickler	Nov. 4

Born after Grandma's death

1978	Kathy Strickler	May 3
1981	Brandon Minor	Sept. 5
1982	Joe Armstrong, Jr.	June 26
1982	Steven Minor	Oct. 7
1983	Sue Armstrong	July 13
1983	Amber Yates	Oct. 15
1984	Heather Turner	Aug. 20
1986	Kimberly Yates	Feb. 6
1987	Holly Turner	Aug. 11
1987	Duncan Yates	Oct. 20

EIGHTH GENERATION

Their Great-great grandchildren (5)

1997	Zach Strickler	April 14
1998	Junior McMurrin	Dec. 6
2003	Natalie Dant	Dec. 3
2003	Jacinda Ireland	Jan. 1
2005	Jamal Ireland	April 8

The "Grand Kids"

1956. Eileen and the three Minor sons: David 12, Mark 8, and Neil 5. Elaine was born on Christmas Eve. Dad is Maurice Minor.

1958. Pam 1 and Allen 5 are children of George and Darlene Strong. Both adults are now employed in Cedar Rapids; Pam has two daughters. She assumed her maiden name after divorce.

1963. Janice 8, Rick 5, Steve 2, and Karen 1, in their Cedar Rapids home. Parents are Norman and Doris Neal. [Their youngest, Karen Yates McVeigh, has three children: her youngest, Kim, married Chris Dant, who is returning to Iraq for 2nd tour with US Army. They have a daughter, Natalie.]

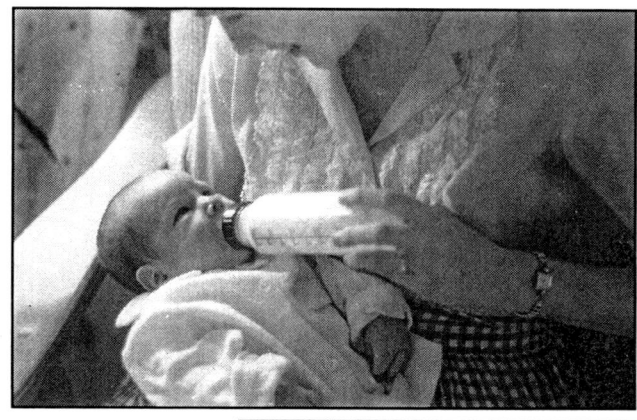

1958. Ruth Ann feeds her baby Joey in California.

2007. Leslie Strickler and her two sons, Junior 8, and Zack 10, on a visit with her grandparents (Norman and Doris Neal) in Swisher for a cookout.
Leslie's parents: Joe and Janice Neal Strickler.

2005. Kathy Strickler works as Senior Mall Accountant, Jordan Creek Town Center, West Des Moines. Graduate, Mount Mercy College, Cedar Rapids, 2004. Parents: Joe and Janice Strickler.

1992. Sue, 9, and Joe Armstrong, Jr., 10. Parents: Joe and Susie Armstrong. Parents, children and grandchildren live in Florida. Both children are working adults.

"Grand children" not pictured above may paste his/her photo to the right.

YOUR PHOTO HERE

Grandpas & Grandmas

1920s. Thelma's parents, Samuel E. and Mary E. Oliver at their Indiana farm. He died in Indiana in 1931. She died at the Mount Vernon, Iowa farm in 1944.

1911. Walter's parents and grandfather George A., 41, Henry G., 77, and Nettie Bowman Strong.

1909. The George A. Strong family wintering in Pasadena, CA. From left, George, Dale B., Walter B. with dog, and Nettie.

This Copy of "Never Say Never" belongs to

_____

Contents

Front Matter
Family Tree iv
About Our Ancestors 1
Dedication to the "Grand Kids" 3
Grandpas & Grandmas 7

I Recalling My Life, Thelma Strong 11
    Honors Student in Indianapolis 12
    Joins Family in Cedar Rapids 15
    Meets Walter Strong 16
    Elopes in 1921 18
    The Marion Farm 19
    The "Little House" (1922-1936) 20
    Friends and Visitors 25
    A Growing Family 27
    The "Big House" (1936-1940) 29
    Mount Vernon Farm (1940-1945) 31
    Returns to Cedar Rapids 32
    Children Grow Up 34
    Financial Matters 38
    Entertaining in Cedar Rapids Home 40
    Retires to Downtown Apartment 41

II Letter from Mae (Smith) Peterson 45
    The Big House Described 47

III Thelma's Travels 49

IV Excerpts from Thelma's Letters 53

V Remembering Our Parents, Jean Strong 55

VI Afterword 59
    Dates of Family Member Deaths 60
    Value of $1.00 in Selected Years 61
    Index of Family Names 62
    Life of a Family in 20th Century Linn County 66

1956. Grandma Strong with her first six grandkids: Baby Elaine, Neil 4, David 11, Mark 7, Janice Neal 8 months, and Allen Strong 2, at Minor farm northwest of Manchester.

1954. Grandma Strong with Allen Strong, 1.

1956. Elaine Minor, sixth grandchild of Thelma Strong, whoops it up in her play pen (above). Undoubtedly the most amiable of Thelma's grandchildren, then and now, Elaine (left, 2005) is a commercial mortgage loan closing specialist at AEGON USA Realty Advisors in Cedar Rapids.

1956. Grandma Thelma Strong rides mule into Grand Canyon.

I
Recalling My Life
Thelma Strong

I WAS BORN at our home on March 13, 1900 at 3:15 p.m. My parents, Samuel Ellsworth and Mary Elizabeth (Morgan) Oliver, lived in an apartment above a grocery store in Brightwood, a suburb in Indianapolis, Indiana. The store was at Pendleton Pike and Gale Street. I was the ninth of 11 children. A brother and a sister had died as babies.

My six living sisters and brothers were Ethel 20, Evvie 18, Blanche 12, Clyde 10, Anna 7, and Sherman 5. Two more sisters—Gladys and Dora—were yet to be born at two-year intervals. Soon after I arrived, my Dad bought a house nearby. The address was 2510 Walker Street, just off Pendleton Pike, and we lived here until I was 13.

Honors Student in Indianapolis

My formal schooling began, when I was six, at James Russell Lowell grade school in Brightwood. I graduated with honors from the eighth grade June 19, 1915. I thought I would be nervous giving my address about the Panama Canal as part of the commencement program, but I wasn't.

Before I was born, my Dad served during the Spanish-American War (Cuba) for nearly 10 months. He served in Company D, 161st Indiana Volunteer Infantry, from July 5, 1898 until his discharge on April 30, 1899.

> [Samuel's great-great-great grandfather, George Oliver, and four of his 10 sons, served in the Revolutionary War at the Battle of the Guilford County Courthouse in North Carolina. (Oliver, Hugh R. and Margaret T., 1987, "Sketches of the Olivers, A Family History 1726 to 1966.")]

Dad was 42 when I was born and my memory of his work was as a railroader and carpenter, and later a farmer. In Indiana, he operated a derrick for the Big Four Railroad. Salvaging a wrecked train often kept him away from home for a week at a time. From our home, we could hear the wreck whistle that alerted him of a mishap, and away he would go with a crew to pick up spilled freight.

I took piano lessons from Blythe Bowman. She was not a good teacher because she never taught the correct fingering but, as a young woman, I enjoyed playing for family and friends.

In March of 1913, my Dad's job with the Big Four took us to Peru, Indiana for a year. Evvie, Ray, Sherman, Dad and I moved to the new home, but my sister Annie Finneran, now 20 and married, was expecting a baby, and our mother (Mary Oliver) stayed behind to help her. Annie's first daughter, Mary Finneran, was born March 8, 1913.

Shortly after we arrived at our Peru home on top of a big hill, water came to within two blocks of our house and flooded the town below. Water seeped into the basement, preventing us from using the furnace; we used a wood stove for heat and for cooking. The gas, normally used for cooking, was off, too.

> (On the Wabash River, Peru endured its last and worst flood, cresting at more than 25 feet on March 26, 1913, before the dams were installed. Eleven people lost their lives.)

I attended school for the year in Peru and liked Mr. Grump, my teacher. After 10 months, my Dad's work with the railroad was finished and, in December 1913, we moved back to our home place on Walker Street in Indianapolis where we remained for the next 11 months.

My two brothers served in the armed services during World War I. Clyde enlisted in the Army on December 26, 1913, and was discharged from Camp Knox, Kentucky, on July 20, 1920. He served with a supply company, 83rd Field Artillery.

Sherman (John S.) enlisted July 29, 1918 in Cedar Rapids, and was scheduled to go overseas in November but became ill with pneumonia while in New York City and did not get to go. Dad got an emergency railroad pass for both parents to go visit him. Sherman was discharged June 20, 1919 at Des Moines, Iowa, from B210 Company of Engineers.

In November 1914, my folks moved to Cedar Rapids, where Dad and two brothers-in-law found jobs at the Rock Island Railroad yards repairing boxcars. My sister Evvie had married Ray Thoroughman, and our sister Ethel married Frank Payton.

When my folks left Indiana, I stayed behind to finish the eighth grade. My sister Annie was expecting another baby so I stayed with the Finnerans to help. The baby girl, Eileen, was born December 16, 1914, and on January 3, 1915, I went to live with my Aunt Agnes and Uncle George Morgan on Adams Street, only two blocks from my school. Uncle George was my mother's youngest brother; they had lived with us for a time when I was a baby. Aunt Agnes, whose own baby had died, was like a mother to me.

1915. Thelma at 8th grade graduation in Indiana with teacher Bertha Ebbert and Alice Sickle (Bouches).

1919. Thelma's home from 1916 to September 1919 is at J Avenue and 11th Street in northeast Cedar Rapids. An employed bookkeeper, she remains in Iowa when her parents return to Indiana. She wrote on back of photo, "Grandpa Oliver built the log house in 1916, using trees from the lot."

Joins Family in Cedar Rapids

After graduating, I came to Cedar Rapids and, in the fall of 1915, entered Old Washington High School where I took English, shorthand, typing and bookkeeping. The following year, I joined the Daniel's Park Presbyterian Church on 13th Street, northeast Cedar Rapids—not far from our home on Eleventh Street.

I met the Martin Smith family and became good friends with their daughters Viola, Zelma, May, Ivadine, Bernice and Dorothy. Their three sons were Q, Roy, and Marty, Jr.

In November 1915, two months after starting high school, I got a job at Kresge's Five & Ten Cents Store. I went to school in the mornings and worked at a counter selling kerosene lamps and gas shades, from 1 to 6 p.m., Monday through Friday, and from 8 to 10 on Saturdays. My wage was $2.65 a week.

> [One 1915 dollar has buying power of $20.64 in 2007, according to the Inflation Calculator at Bureau of Labor statistics web site, www.bls.gov.]

At that time, movies were five cents; ice cream cones two for five cents, and chocolates 20 cents a pound. My mother made dresses for me from material I bought with my earnings.

Only a week before the end of my first year, I quit school and began working full time. I carried lunch and took the entire hour to eat my apple and one sandwich; I had learned in hygiene class at school to eat slowly and chew thoroughly before swallowing.

I now earned $4.50 a week by working five days from 8 to 6, and 8 a.m. to 10 p.m. on Saturdays.

> [1916 dollar would buy $19.13 in 2007.]

I worked in hosiery, at the greeting card counters, and the fruit stand. George Kaiser, whose shoe store was next door to Kresge's, came in nearly every day and I had fun trying to sell him the many Saturday specials the store offered to assist the staff in making extra sales.

We blew water through toy metal birds with a pipe attached to make the store sound atwitter with canaries. Many people bought them. Another time, the special was men's neckties for 10 and 20 cents.

When Mr. Kaiser asked me to work at his shoe store, I gave Kresge's notice and on September 19, 1917 started as his bookkeeper and cashier, replacing a departing bookkeeper. He started me at $7.50, the same weekly salary I was making at Kresge's.

[1917 dollar equals $16.29 in 2007.]

I walked to work taking a shortcut along the railroad tracks. It was about one mile from home to work and sometimes, during rainstorms, I arrived at the shoe store soaked below my coat from the knees down.

In November 1918, when my brother Sherman was sick with pneumonia in New York City, I bought my mother a coat and a hat to wear on the trip to visit him.

Meets Walter Strong

One Saturday night in November of 1919, a young man named Walter Strong came into the store to buy a pair of overshoes. Walter's stepmother was Mr. Kaiser's sister-in-law. Mr. Kaiser introduced us and Walter went down to the basement where the overshoes were on display. A customer came in to pick up shoes he had left for repair and I went to the basement to get them.

Mr. Kaiser's brother, Abbie, who ran the repair shop, started teasing me about making a date with Walter. Shy Walter stood by, grinning. We visited and I told him my friend, Viola Smith, and I were planning to take a long walk the next day and I agreed that we would walk to Marion where Walter said he and a friend would meet us at Mr. Kaiser's home on Sixth Avenue.

That Sunday afternoon, Viola and I walked the three miles to the Kaiser residence in Marion. Walter came in his 1916 two-seat Ford, bringing his friend, Harold Vahl, as promised. The boys brought us back to Cedar Rapids so we did not have to walk or ride the streetcar that connected the two cities.

[Marion was the county seat from 1839 until an election in 1919 awarded the courthouse to Cedar Rapids.]

I am not sure, but think we may have gone to church, as Viola and I usually did, and then went to my home.

At that time, I lived with my sister Evvie Thoroughman, her husband Ray and son Raymond.

Over the next few years, four or five couples continued to get together for parties and picnics. I often played piano and we sang. We danced, too, but not at the Smith home because Mr. Smith did not approve.

1920. Walter Strong and Thelma Oliver pose while courting at Ray and Evvie Thoroughman home she shared on Wenig Road NE, Cedar Rapids.

Before meeting Walter, I dated a Coe student preacher named Herman Humke, and a man named Leonard Hill—both friends I met at church. I broke off with Leonard after four or five dates because by then I was dating Walter and did not want to date two fellows at once. I was working the same hours at Kaiser's as I had at the dime store. Earlier, Mr. Humke had proposed by letter and wanted me to go to Chicago with him, but I was not interested.

In September 1919, my folks moved back to Indiana after living four years in the log house my Dad built in Cedar Rapids. Before they left, he put siding on the house so he could sell it.

Mr. Kaiser promised me three weeks' vacation at Christmas so I could go to Indiana to be with my family. He kept his word and Walter and I corresponded. While I was away, Walter went to parties with our friends at the church, and when I returned in January of 1920, he and our friends met me at the train.

Walter and I stood up with my sister Gladys when she married Roy Byerly on June 24, 1920. We had a picnic that evening. By

September, we decided to get married, too, but Walter wanted to keep it secret from his parents. They knew we were dating; we often ate Sunday supper with them in the big house on the farm when Walter went home to do the chores. Walter was not yet 21.

Elopes in 1921

I told Mr. Kaiser I wanted to go home to Indiana for a week, and Walter and I eloped to Vinton. Sister Evvie and little Raymond went with us. Judge Burnham married us at the Benton County Courthouse on October 6, 1921.

Walter's one-seat Ford roadster broke down on the way back a few miles west of Cedar Rapids; we hitched a ride with a Laurence Cook crockery salesman. Evvie and Raymond rode up front with the driver, and Walter and I rode in back on top of four hundred dollars worth of cut glass dishes. The salesman asked if we were newlyweds.

After our marriage, I lived in a spare bedroom at the Byerlys. Gladys and Roy were living with his mother. About two months later, Walter told Miss Ramsey, the woman who worked for his parents, that he was married. She said, "Why, you little devil, you!" She told Mr. and Mrs. Strong and then we announced our marriage in the paper. Just after that, I became pregnant with Eileen, our first-born.

> [A wedding announcement which came as a surprise to many friends was that of Miss Thelma Oliver of this city, daughter of Mr. and Mrs. S. E. Oliver of Indianapolis, and Walter B. Strong of Marion. The wedding took place in Vinton on Oct. 6, 1921.]

The Marion Farm

1936. Looking southeast from little house to the big house and garage, clockwise, Eileen 14, Jean 11, George 9, Doris Mae 4, Ruth Ann 6 mos. Below, winter 1938, the little house and windmill in background as three Strong children, and the son of hired man Albert Stark, shovel two-feet of snow from big house driveway.

The "Little House" (1922-1936)

Mr. Strong had started tearing down the old nine-room home on the farm where Walter was born. He planned to convert the house into a corncrib. On learning of our marriage, he decided to fix up the house for us to live in. Walter and I moved into the little house on April 11, 1922.

I had never lived on a farm, and always said I would never marry a farmer, but Walter was the only man I ever saw that I wanted. I fell in love and was never sorry that I married a farmer after all. And I learned never to say 'never.'

In 1922, while we were living in the little house on the Marion farm, we visited back and forth with our near neighbors, the John Eppersons. They gave us a lift to Marion each Saturday night to get our week's groceries during the period when we did not have a car of our own.

When they planned on going to town during the week, they invited us to go along by hanging a white cloth on the clothesline and then stopped that evening to pick us up.

This signaling was more convenient than going to the big house to receive or make a telephone call. We did not have a telephone in our little house. Our farm was one mile north of Marion and the Eppersons lived a half mile north of us.

The Eppersons and their son, Lyle, moved to Lincoln, Illinois in the early 1920s. John died a few years ago and his wife, Alpha, moved to town from their acreage. Now in her eighties, her hair is still very dark, no gray hairs.

1923. Thelma wrote caption on back of the photo: "Me and my bobbed hair, Eileen 1, and Mr. Strong by his Nash the day we went fishing at Troy Mills."

After Eileen arrived on August 31, 1922, it seemed the house got dark awfully early and I was a little uneasy about being alone until Walter came in from doing chores. It was usually 6:30 or 7 o'clock before he came in to eat after finishing all of the chores, including the milking.

1926. Thelma with Eileen and Jean one Sunday in Bever Park.

Eileen had the colic for six weeks after she was born and I had to hold her on my hip while I fixed supper. In the early days of our marriage, I cooked on a new, four-burner kerosene stove.

With the fifty dollars Mr. Strong gave us for a wedding present, we bought a second-hand square dining table, six chairs, dishes from the dime store, and some flatware knives, forks and spoons.

[A 1922 dollar would buy $12.41 in 2007.]

Other furnishings for our home were also second-hand. They included a washstand with a mirror that we bought for six dollars, an iron bedstead and mattress from my sister Evvie, and a rocking chair that Walter picked up at an auction sale for one dollar.

Grandpa and "Auntie" Strong gave us an old rug for the living room and a washstand for the kitchen where we all washed up.

[Walter's mother, Nettie, died in 1914 when he was 13.
The second Mrs. Strong (Ida Crowley) did not wish to be called 'Grandma.']

We did not have indoor plumbing, but we did have an electric-operated pump at our back door with good-tasting, ice-cold well water. A windmill powered the pump when the wind blew.

For heating the house, we had a big pot belly old stove that had been out in the barn. We used it in the kitchen the first year or two until we bought a new heating stove for the other room. In winter, we took tub baths near the stove; the children remember toasting on one side and freezing on the other.

In the spring, we made a garden and I did most of the work although Walter helped when he could. I never worked outside other than in the garden and in the yard where I had flowers. Our garden was the section north of the patch between the big house and the barn.

We also raised chickens and sometimes I helped feed them—especially when they were little. We always bought 50 one-day-old chicks and, because we were interested in eating them eventually, we tried to get mostly all roosters.

Our first vacation was in 1924 when Walter, Eileen and I went by train to my parents' home in Indiana for the Christmas holidays. We stayed two weeks.

Jean was born July 19, 1925 and, during the winter of that year, Grandpa Strong and Auntie went to California. They had us live in the big house for about four months so they would not have to drain the pipes. Jean pulled off some of the loose wallpaper from above the heaters. Perhaps the memory of that fun is why she scooted across our driveway the following summer, heading for the big house. She scooted rather than crawled before she walked.

In the early Twenties, I was glad to get, finally, a good cook stove. Our neighbors and friends, the Eppersons, were moving to Illinois. Although they had paid more than one hundred dollars for the stove a few months earlier, they sold it to us for $45.00. It was a Junger and had a reservoir for hot water, and an overhead warming oven to keep food hot. *[Nearly $500 value in 2007.]*

The stove never required black stove polish. It would shine like new when I applied some lard on a cloth and rubbed it over the warm surface. It was a six-hole range and we burned wood in it. After Grandpa Strong died in 1936, we moved to the big house and I sold the stove to my sister Dora.

In 1926, when Marthella Schmidt and her mother were selling their household furnishings, we bought their drop-leaf desk for $5.00, an old library table, and a Thor washing machine. Before that, I had washed on the washboard and then boiled the clothes in the wash boiler as my mother had done.

[1926 dollar value is $11.78 in 2007.]

Before George was born April 21, 1928, we bought a new brown leather davenport that made into a bed and Eileen and Jean slept on that. We had a crib for George. Just before he was born, we bought a four-drawer chest new for $20.00 *[2007, $244]*, two iron beds and coil springs. We had bought an icebox new and the crib after Eileen was born.

George cried a lot when he was first born because he was not getting enough to eat from me. After I started feeding him on the bottle, he stopped crying. He was a big baby—9½ pounds and 22 inches long.

When we were expecting our fourth child in 1929, we were still living in two large rooms—the kitchen and combination living-bedroom. Before the new baby arrived, Mr. Strong finished off two upstairs bedrooms. Born on December 17, Patricia Ann died on December 30, 1929. We still had our first three children, Eileen, Jean and George—and a bigger house.

In August of 1930, we took a three-week vacation in our 1927 Chevrolet, with the three children. My folks had had their 50th wedding anniversary on December 25, 1929, but we had not had a family celebration then. At the time, my mother was with us on the farm awaiting the arrival of our fourth child, Patricia Ann, who died 13 days after she was born. We had sent money so my Dad could come to Iowa for Christmas, and planned the family get-together for the coming summer to observe their anniversary in Indiana.

1930. Eileen, Jean, and George with their mom and dad on a Sunday visit with the Art Craft family in northeast Cedar Rapids.

1932. Jean hugs visitor Ray Bouches in snapshot with George (center) and Eileen holding two-month old Doris Mae. The big house is in right background.

After Doris Mae was born on July 1, 1932, George pestered my mother when she was bathing the new baby. "George, why don't you go in and rock and listen to 'Happy Jack Turner' on the radio," she suggested. Happy Jack was a radio entertainer who played piano. George would go sit in the little red rocker and rock for an hour or two at a time; he was four.

Alice Bouches, my schoolchild chum in Indiana, came from California with her son, Ray, to visit us for a few days in 1932. We have kept in touch on birthdays and at Christmas through the years. Her first husband, Bill Schaar, died while they were living in Chicago. She later moved to California and married Raymond Bouches. Her maiden name was Sickle. She and Ray had two sons, Raymond and Bill. Although Alice is now blind, she has adjusted well and seems happy. She lives in Fresno, California.

Friends and Visitors

Before Alice Bouches' visit from California, our most frequent visitors were my sisters and brothers, and our friends. Viola Smith Matteson often came on weekends with her daughter, Mildred, and Marthella Schmidt and Mae Smith came, too.

> [Mildred always recalled the delicious fried potatoes Thelma made in her big iron skillet on the Junger range.]

In 1915, when I first came to Cedar Rapids, a young man was building a home on the avenue behind our house for his bride. His name was Art Craft, and he and Gladys became our friends. They had three children, a son and two daughters, Helen and Marilyn. We exchanged Sunday visits. Art died a few years ago, but Gladys still lives in northeast Cedar Rapids.

The Smith family remained our friends through the years also. Zelma married Roy Finson in 1921 and lived on a farm at Central City near where she had been teaching school. *[They later moved to a farm near Monticello.]* We spent many Sundays and holidays with them and enjoyed many delicious meals and good times together. Both have since died but their two children, Dorothy Finson Christensen and Dick Finson, are still living out-of-state.

Mae Smith did not marry until she was 40. Her husband is Henry Peterson, an attorney in Chicago. They had two children of their own (Patty and Peter) and several foster children.

Viola married George Matteson in 1922, and they and their two children were our neighbors in northeast Cedar Rapids before they became our first renters. He traveled as an accountant for D-X Oil Company; she worked at Armstrong's department store as a sales person in women's wear. She died in 1977.

When Eileen started going to Picayune country school in 1928, we met the Donald Atwater family. Their son, George, and daughter, Isabelle, were pupils, and later their son, Harold, attended school along with our other children. Ruth Ann is the only one of our children who did not attend Picayune.

1936. Retired from the Elmer Graham farm, Lady spends her final months at the Marion farm with the appreciative Strong children.

1937. Atwater-Strong picnic. Ethel Atwater took the photo of husband Don, Walter, Thelma, Isabelle Atwater, Eileen; (front) Doris Mae, George, Jean, Harold Atwater and Ruth Ann.

A Growing Family

George was born on April 21, 1928 and was our only son. It was a cold day in July when Doris Mae was born on July 1, 1932, and she was only two when a dust and windstorm came up on July 4, 1934. It was so sudden; I ran to close the windows of the house. It scared Doris Mae and she was always afraid of storms after that. George, only six, had been out back in the outhouse and he came running. It blew over after he left it.

It was another cold day when Ruth Ann was born on January 9, 1936. My mother kept Jean and George outside the house until the baby came at 8:15 a.m. Eileen stayed upstairs with Doris. Eileen, Jean and George then went to school with the proud news that they had a new baby sister.

Dr. W. E. Brown, who delivered all of my children in the little house, returned the next day on the tenth. A big snowstorm came after he left and drifted fence-high all across the roads. Although the road was passable for the mile from town to our farm, the doctor did not come out again.

> [Dr. Brown was a practicing physician and teaching obstetrician at St. Luke's Hospital following a distinguished career in the U.S. Medical Corps. His death occurred several years after delivering Ruth Ann Strong.]

The road was closed going north and the three children had a holiday from the Picayune country school that was one and three-quarter miles north on the Alburnett Road.

That winter was so cold I worried that the new baby would freeze. It was 28 degrees below part of the time. I kept Ruth Ann wrapped up in her crib and close to the heating stove.

My mother came to help a few weeks before each of my children was born and stayed until the babies were three weeks old. We always borrowed train fare from Walter's dad for her to come, and he added it to what we owed.

Mr. Strong charged us for one-fourth of all the livestock, feed and grain he purchased for the 200-acre farm. He subtracted expenses from what he paid us after selling cattle or hogs.

1936. Last photo of Grandpa Strong with his automobile, and Doris Mae, Auntie, George, Jean, Eileen, Cousin Eileen Leinen and Grandma Mary Oliver. Aviator helmets are in fashion for 7-year-old George and Jean 10.

1937. Visiting cousins at the big house, from left, Eileen Leinen, Marion; George, Jean holding Ruth Ann Strong, Bob Byerly 12, Eileen Strong, Mary Byerly holding Johnny 2. Three youngsters in front: George 6 and Ellsworth Byerly 9, and Doris Mae Strong.

The "Big House" (1936-1940)

It was a hot summer in 1936 and Walter's dad was seriously ill with a heart condition. He died on October 7. Ida, his widow, moved to town (*Marion*) to live with her sister, Mrs. George Kaiser, and we moved down into the big house on November 30.

1937. Grandpa Strong's big house was our home for more than three years, November 1936 to February 1940. The G. A. Strong Estate was finally settled after Adolph Boyson bought the farm.

1938. October. On visit from Indiana, Aunt Agnes photographed the Strong family posing below the second-floor sleeping porch and outside the den and dining room windows downstairs.

1938. Thelma wrote on back of this photo, "Here we are; just came in with load of corn. I helped. Ha ha." Jean, 13, used her mother's Kodak box camera to photograph family with final load.

Living in the big house cost a lot more than the little one where we had lived for 15 years. Coal was twenty dollars a ton or more. We bought the better grades because the cheaper kind was so dirty and made a lot of soot. It was nice to have a bathroom—our first—and running hot and cold water upstairs and down.

[A 1937 dollar is valued at $14.48 in 2007.]

In 1939, we sold the farm to Adolph Boyson, a Cedar Rapids' jeweler, and continued to live there while harvesting our crops. He came out and walked around the farm shaking the fence posts loose, and then he would tell Walter they needed replacing. He often stayed and ate supper with us and seemed to enjoy it much more than restaurant food.

His wife had died, and after he purchased the farm, he converted part of the upstairs' bedrooms and the sleeping porch into an apartment for himself. He paid Eileen one dollar for cleaning it once a week. Jean took care of his young racehorse (Prince Medair) daily for one dollar a week.

[1939 dollar value is $15.00 in 2007.]

He paid me thirty-five cents a meal *[$5.25 today value]* when he ate with us and he enjoyed my tapioca pudding the most, but seemed to enjoy being with our family. When my Mom gave me a set of Nobility silverware for Christmas in 1939, she had not bought tablespoons; Mr. Boyson gave me three nice Gorham silver ones.

Mount Vernon Farm (1940-1945)

We bought the 120-acre farm near Mt. Vernon in July of 1939 and moved there in February 1940 after holding a sale to settle the George Strong estate. His widow and two sons were heirs. We lived on the Mount Vernon farm for nearly six years.

Walter's health was bad, and he started working in Cedar Rapids at Quaker Oats in April 1945. Ray Martin farmed the land that year and we sold the farm to him on June 19 for $19,000 *[$158.33 an acre]*. We had paid $15,000 ($125/acre).

1942. Strong children sit on sled in front yard of nine-room Mount Vernon farm home. From left: Eileen 20, Jean 17 holding dog, George 14, Doris Mae 10 and Ruth Ann 6.

Returns to Cedar Rapids

1947. Strong family at 149 33rd Street NE, Cedar Rapids home in December while Jean was home for the holidays from the University of Iowa.

1948. Exterior front of "149" after finishing the upstairs. Thelma worked with Carl Stark, a master carpenter, in creating a three-bedroom apartment with kitchen, living room, and ample storage.

1951. Entrance to new downstairs' room improved backyard appearance. Enclosed apartment stairway was added in 1947.

We purchased the house at 149 33rd Street NE, Cedar Rapids, in July 1945, and moved there December 7.

[A 1945 dollar would purchase $11.58 in 2007.]

Walter never liked farming but his dad needed him so we had stayed on. At Quaker, he helped load boxcars with 100-pound sacks of feed and enjoyed it for a little more than two and one-half years before he had to give it up.

In December 1947, he had the flu and it seemed to hang on until he was admitted to St. Luke's Hospital on January 12, 1948. He remained in the hospital for six and one-half weeks until February 23, 1948. The hospital bill was more than $700 and Blue Cross paid for most of it; we paid a little more than one hundred dollars.

[1948 dollar is worth $8.65 in 2007.]

In August of 1948, George took Walter and me to Indiana for a week in his new Dodge. It was used, but new to him *(and replaced his first car, a Model-T Ford)*. The Dodge was a nice car, and we stayed for a week with my Aunt Agnes and Uncle George Morgan and visited my sisters, nieces and nephews in and around Indianapolis.

The following year, August 1949, Dr. J.J. Keith said Walter could drive to Indiana if we would take two days and stop overnight, so we took our fourth and last vacation together. It was before school was to start and we took Ruth Ann and Doris Mae with us and stayed with Aunt Agnes and Uncle George again. *[Walter had bought his first and only new car, a 1950 Dodge. He drove that on this trip.]*

Then, in November, Dr. Keith had Walter admitted to University Hospital in Iowa City for tests. He was there for two weeks until just before Thanksgiving. Jean was attending the university. Walter returned to work for a few days after that but soon had to stay home.

Children Grow Up

Eileen had attended Business College in Cedar Rapids and worked for several years in Cedar Rapids. She married Maurice Minor in 1942 while we lived on the Mt. Vernon farm. Maurice joined the Navy and Eileen continued working in Cedar Rapids.

On December 7, 1944, David was born and we all were so happy to have our first grandchild. His dad got home on leave for Christmas and saw him for the first time. World War II ended in August 1945 and Maurice came home in November.

Jean graduated from Springville High in 1943, and took a job at the *Marion Sentinel* to learn linotyping. By 1945, she had saved enough money to start college. She graduated from the school of journalism at the University of Iowa on February 3, 1951, and we all attended the graduation ceremony.

She went to work on February 5, 1951 at the *Cedar Rapids Gazette* until April 1954 when she moved to New York City to work for *Life* magazine.

> [Jean joined *Fortune* magazine in 1960; returned to Cedar Rapids 1962, moved to Philadelphia 1971, and to Washington, D.C. in 1973.]

George had finished eighth grade when we moved to Cedar Rapids. He worked at Quaker Oats for a while and then went to the Colonial Bakery; he has been in their employ since except for two years when he worked at Fruehaupt's and then at Dows' Dairy farm for a short time before returning to the bakery.

George and Darlene Moser were married in Cedar Rapids on May 10, 1952. Allen was born March 16, 1953, and Pam on December 12, 1957. They lived with me from April 1957 until 1960 before Ruth Ann remarried. *[George retired from the bakery in 1990.]*

Doris Mae worked at Craemer's Dry Goods store after graduating from Franklin High in 1953, and married Norman Neal on April 28, 1954. They lived with me for two years to help me by renting the two rooms in my big house. Norman worked at reading water meters, and later went to work as a mail carrier at the Post Office. He went back to reading meters before getting into the carpet laying business and later became his own boss.

> [The Neals had a home in northwest Cedar Rapids before moving to Swisher in March 1964.]

Ruth Ann graduated from Franklin High in 1954. She married Stan Mazgay April 6, 1957, and Joey was born in California on June 2, 1958. After Ruth and Stan divorced in October of 1958, Ruth Ann returned to Cedar Rapids with Joey and worked at Collins Radio where she met John Armstrong. They were married July 26, 1960, and John adopted Joey.

> [As a young U.S. Navy recruit, John was aboard the *USS Oklahoma,* one of the ships sunk at Pearl Harbor on December 7, 1941.]

The Armstrongs lived with me until they bought a house in Walford and sold it before moving to Lake Worth, Florida in 1968.

1966. The Maurice Minor family gathers at Wartburg College, Waverly, for oldest son David's graduation. From left, Maurice, Elaine (graduate U. of Northern Iowa 1978), Eileen, Mark (B.S. 1979 Montana State U. after 5 years in Air Force), and Neil (longtime employee at a back hoe manufacturing facility in Delhi).

1952. August. Darlene and George Strong enjoy her birthday celebration with other family members (Doris holding Neil, Mark and David Minor, and Ruth). The two Strong children born later (Allen and Pam) live and work in Cedar Rapids.

1966. December. Norman and Doris Neal with their four children, Janice, Rick, Steve, and Karen. Their three surviving children live in Norway (Rick), Iowa City (Steve with wife Melissa), and Wasilla, Alaska (Karen and husband, Steven McVeigh).

1966. John, Ruth and Joe Armstrong, in Cedar Rapids, at Christmas. Two years later, they moved from Walford to Florida.

Financial Matters

In 1947, Walter and I decided to make an apartment on the second floor of our home. Carl Stark did the work for us, finishing in October. Our first renters were George and Viola (Smith) Matteson, their daughter Mildred and son, Robert. Viola was my girlhood friend. Rent for the three-bedroom apartment was seventy dollars a month.

Total cost for making the apartment was $3,946.79. We borrowed three thousand dollars from the First National Bank in Marion, and sold some preferred stock in Iowa Electric Light & Power to pay for the labor, material and fixtures.

[1947 dollar value in 2007 is $9.35.]

While working at Quaker Oats, Walter had a sum deducted from his pay each week to purchase U.S. Savings Bonds and we sold them to pay for the new paving in front of our home. The cost for the paving was about $520.00.

In 1951, we added a room downstairs for Jean when she finished college and was starting work at the *Gazette. [Downstairs then had four bedrooms and one bath.]* We still owed eight hundred dollars on the loan for upstairs, and borrowed another three thousand to pay for her room and another small room and hallway to connect her living and bedroom to the bathroom. She paid $100 a month for her room and board that helped as Walter was not able to work.

[1951 dollar is valued at $8.02 in 2007.]

When Walter died in June, I had the two rent incomes and social security for Doris Mae and Ruth Ann until they reached 18 and some for me as a widow while the girls were underage.

> [Walter died of heart disease as stated on the death certificate, but the underlying cause was lupus, Dr. Keith later told Jean.]

The Mattesons moved to their new home on Oakland Avenue in northeast Cedar Rapids in October of 1951, and over the next 18 years, nineteen renters occupied the apartment. Mrs. Lina Kassel, No. 7, and her two daughters, Katy and Joanne, were there from January 1956 until April 1960. She married Norman Chase who also worked at Collins Radio and they moved to Texas when Collins transferred him to the Richardson plant.

Mrs. Lavonne Williams, her daughter Kay Marsh, and granddaughter, Beth, were No. 13 renters—from June 1966 to February 1969 when LaVonne married Lyle McElrath and moved to his home on the west side of Cedar Rapids.

My daughter, Jean, became the 16th renter in 1971-72 while she was in the insurance business and before she moved to Philadelphia as an associate editor for *Farm Journal*. Mrs. Grace Driscoll, a private nurse, was still in the apartment as No. 19 renter when I sold the house to the Greens on September 5, 1973.

The other 14 renters stayed from two to four months and little more than a year. By name they were the Larry Nuss family, Mrs. Joyce Lowry and daughter Joyce, Bob Bensons, Oscar Swensons, the Thomas', Doug and Shirley Holets, Dean and Gale Beer, the Bergmans, Jack Wiseharts, Jack Ohls, Conrad Meyers, Elmer Kellys, Mike Mastain, Mike Conrad (two bad renters), before Mrs. Driscoll.

I baby sat for the Holets and Beer families, and kept my grandson Joey from 1958 until 1961 when Ruth Ann and John moved to Walford.

Entertaining in Cedar Rapids Home

1953. Thelma and daughters entertain German visitors and friends (from left) Lois Emanuel, pharmacist; Journalist Christa Braun of Stuttgart, Connie Polasky, Ruth, Thelma, Doris, 2nd German, Naomi Doebel, Gazette editor, and Edna Herbst, KCRG radio and TV. Jean met the German visitors at the *Gazette*. Their post-war tour was sponsored by the U.S. State Department.

1958. Christmas Eve at Grandma's is a family tradition until Thelma sold the family home in 1973. Gift opening followed dinner. From left, Mark, Joey, Elaine, Neil, Allen, Pam and Janice.

Retires to Downtown Apartment

I had applied for a room at Geneva Tower and was on the waiting list there. On September 29, 1973, I moved in with George and Darlene in northeast Cedar Rapids. Their daughter, Pam, shared her room with me. On December 16, we (George and family) left for Florida to visit Ruth Ann's family and I stayed on until January 12, 1974 when I went by train to Washington, D.C. I visited Jean for two months—until March 22 of that year.

1973. Christmas in Florida with the Armstrongs. Clockwise, Thelma, Darlene, Jean, Pam, Joe Armstrong, Allen, John and Ruth Armstrong. George Strong took the photo.

Doris Mae called in February and said Geneva Tower had an apartment for me. I had given her power of attorney so she made the deposit required to hold the apartment. I returned to George's home on March 23 and moved into Geneva Tower in downtown Cedar Rapids, my present home, March 30, 1974. I love it here.

The Presbytery of the Presbyterian Church built Geneva Tower for the elderly. The monthly rent when I moved in was $99.00; it was soon raised to $115.00, then to $129.00. In the fall of 1976, we reported our income, health expenses and financial status to the management so they could figure our rents according to our incomes. My rent was lowered considerably. That made me happy because my income is fixed by my social security check and monthly payment from the sale of our home. Present top rent for my apartment is $144.00. Phone service is extra.

[1977 dollar value is $3.44 in 2007.]

Apartments elsewhere are much higher. People here are very nice, most of them, and do not bother me. Each of us has privacy that I like since I have many things I hope to accomplish before my time comes. I enjoy sewing, writing letters and watch some TV, mostly news—and one soap opera, "As the World Turns." I enjoy it. It started back in 1956, I believe, so I must not be the only viewer.

> [The night before she died at St. Luke's Hospital, she watched her Saturday night favorite music show, Lawrence Welk.]

1974. On Oct. 15, Thelma entertains longtime friends, the Smith sisters, at her apartment. From left, Viola Matteson, Ivadene Bergquist, Dorothy Mackey, Mae Peterson and, in front, Bernice Felwock. Ivadene and Mae came from Wisconsin and Chicago.

I love to bake and my friends here keep asking when I will make more kolaches *(Bohemian sweet rolls with fruit or cottage cheese and nut centers)*. I have invited the residents on my floor (fifth) in for kolaches and coffee. The Swangers across the hall bring cake or cookies; another neighbor, Marie Strickland, shares bake-and-serve coffee cakes with me. Anne Kriz often brings delicious sour cream cookies.

I am very thankful to be able to take care of my apartment and myself and love having my family visit whenever they can.

This year has been a busy one with visitors. My sister, Dora Leinen, and her daughter, Eileen, came from California for a week in May; Fran Kelley and her husband, Chris Carson, came from California for two nights in June.

Jean came for my birthday in March, again July 1-5, and September 17-28. She flew from Washington, D.C. twice and drove her car in September. We were working on the family genealogy that she is preparing for publication.

Roy Byerly, his son, Don, and wife stopped for a day, and Roy stayed for dinner in September.

Eileen's two sons were both home for visits but their time overlapped only one day. Mark is in college and working in Bozeman, Montana, and David is working as a photographer for the Los Angeles County Museum in California.

On September 27, a large group of family and friends came to the Geneva Tower to see David and his color slide show that included pictures he took in Hawaii, California, and on his current trip around the United States in New Mexico, Louisiana, Florida, and Washington, D.C. He presented two shows—one for the residents and the second for family and friends.

1982. February. Grandson David Minor in Los Angeles apartment.

Ruth Ann's family visited in July; George and Doris Mae's families are nearby and I see them often. I have 11 wonderful grandchildren and one great granddaughter, Leslie Strickler.

—September 1977
Cedar Rapids, Iowa

Thelma was hospitalized after suffering a heart attack on March 8, 1978. She died five days later on the morning of her 78th birthday, with one daughter (Doris) taking her turn at our mother's bedside. Thelma had lived to see publication of the Strong-Oliver genealogy that she helped prepare but she did not complete the picture albums she was planning for her grandchildren. The following letter about the autobiography—from her friend, Mae Peterson—arrived after Thelma's death.

II
Letter from Mae (Smith) Peterson

Sunday, April 23, 1978

Dear Jean,

    Thank you so much for your mother's autobiography. I was really thrilled with it. It was like living in the past as I remembered so much of it. We were both, or I should say all three of us worked at the dime store at the same time and were all so close. We all had treats after work together. Thelma was so friendly and good to everyone—bless her. We all loved her.

    She tells about her homes. <u>Never</u> did she complain to any of us about them. You will never believe how thrilled I was over the "big" house.* It was beautiful! I walked all over the place repeatedly. I made that a dream. I wanted a house as nice as that one some day and—guess what—mine is as nice but not as large.

    I can remember you more than the others from the time you were tiny going around saying, "Pants are falling down!" And they were, too. Then, of course, when you were still very young you always helped your Dad out of doors. I remember all the children well but it took a long time to believe the two youngest girls were Thelma's as I was in Chicago when they were growing up.

Your Mom was so proud of all of you. In the past few years, she talked about her trip to Chicago with all "my kids." She would say, "How could I do that to you? A whole week!"

We all enjoyed it. You girls all kept track of every penny you spent. It was dreadfully hot and every one helped. Someone took pictures. I guess it was the heat because Thelma wrote me right away how tired I looked. She wrote about it several times in the past two years.

I was so pleased she mentioned our family with such love and regard because that is the way we felt about her.

She was so happy in her little apartment. It was perfect for her. Her trips with and to you meant so much to her. I am so glad she could enjoy them. I wanted her to come here so badly. I'm sure she would have enjoyed it.

Too bad that Vi (Viola) isn't here to give us some more information. Thelma didn't know, I guess, that my dad wouldn't let us play cards at home either. He called them "Devil" cards. Zelma worked at the dime store, too; someone asked her if she carried playing cards and she said, "Do you mean Devil cards?" She was reported to the manager! Can you imagine that? My dad was very religious. However, we danced and played cards elsewhere.

With all my love,
Mae

Mrs. Henry Peterson
Chicago, IL 60631

*The Big House Described

Grandpa George Strong had moved his family into the big house in 1912. It cost $10,000 and was built for show. I believe the same Cedar Rapids architect who designed the James Bowman home on Eighth Avenue, Marion, designed Grandpa's home. The interior finishing is similar although the Big House is on a grander scale. It faced the east and a large lawn extended to the east and south. Two umbrella trees were in front, evergreen trees at the southeast corner and a hedge bordered the Alburnett and West roads. The West Road was later renamed Boyson Road.

Grandpa's favorite room, the den, was in the southwest corner, a large living room extended across the east front of the house, a swinging door separated the dining room from the kitchen which had a walk-in pantry, and enclosed back porch. The telephone on the kitchen wall was a party line; the number was 20-F30.

> [Inflation calculations only began in 1913. A 1913 dollar was worth $9.18 in 1981 when the big house and five acres were listed for sale at $159,950. By 2007, a 1913 dollar was worth $21.]

A player piano graced one end of the long living room and came with the house when our family moved into it in 1936. We kids enjoyed pumping (playing) the music rolls that were kept in a special cabinet. Our Mom kept her sheet music (World War I era) in the music bench and sometimes played for us after supper.

Our living room would have been woefully under-furnished without the overstuffed davenport, rocker and chair set we acquired from Auntie. We later moved the set to the Mount Vernon farm and then to our Cedar Rapids home. The set was not replaced until the early 1960s when our mother finally also got rid of the Persian rugs that "would never wear out," the 1930s salesman had said. They hadn't, but Mom had been sick of them for quite a while.

A rounded plate glass window at the southeast corner of the big house permitted a view of Marion where Grandpa's grandfather,

Luman M. Strong, built the town's first house and inn and lived there along Central Avenue and Indian Creek.

> [Luman Strong was elected one of three county commissioners (supervisors) in 1839. In 1848, he moved his second wife (an Iowa school teacher) and family to Wisconsin where he "read the law," became a state legislator and then was elected Iowa county judge at Dodgeville. One son, Henry G., (George A. Strong's father) came to Iowa from Ohio at age 22 and married Christina Kramer. Henry's mother died in Ohio when he was one year-old.]

A landing between the living room and kitchen of the big house was accessed by steps from each side, and the stairway and second landing, open to the living room, led to the four upstairs bedrooms, bath, and screened sleeping porch that I claimed as my own province although I shared a bedroom with my sister, Eileen. A doorway and steps led to a full attic.

A side-door on the north side of the house opened onto a landing with two sets of stairs—one to the basement and the other up to the right to the kitchen door.

The full basement included a fruit/canned goods storage room with a room for coal, shelves for canned meat and vegetables, ceiling hooks for curing hams, bins for potatoes from the garden and shelves for baskets of apples from the Wealthy apple tree in the south side yard. A furnace supplied central heating, and the shower in the wash room was a convenience that kept barnyard track-in to a minimum.

Quite a change from our partial dirt floor basement and no indoor plumbing at the little house.—*J.S.*

III
Thelma's Travels

"I did enjoy each and every trip and don't know that I could pick out one thing I most enjoyed."—Thelma Strong, 1977.

1952. Thelma and children (George, Doris, Ruth) and Lois Emanuel pose for Jean along Lake Michigan during Chicago visit.

1953. Sisters and brothers gather for the Oliver family reunion at the Byerly home in Indianapolis. From left, Blanche (Mrs. Ed) McCammon, Gladys (Mrs. Roy) Byerly, Clyde Oliver, Dora (Mrs. Al) Leinen, Sherman Oliver, and Thelma Strong.

1952 - To Chicago with my children, and Lois Emanuel. We stayed with Mae Peterson and family for a week.

1956 - To California, Tucson, Arizona and Perkins, Oklahoma, with Ruth Ann and Jean, visiting friends and family.

The trip west, meeting our cousins and seeing my sisters, too, and Aunt Alice. The Hartigs gave Jean $100 for the three of us to ride on mules into the Grand Canyon for overnight at Phantom Ranch. An adventure. Thelma wrote a 20-page report of this trip. Her sister, Dora, was living in California; Blanche in Tucson, Arizona.

1957 - With Jean for *Life's* New England tour. From Iowa we first toured through Indiana, Hampton, Virginia (to visit Raymond Thoroughman and his family) and Williamsburg, Virginia. Jean wanted to establish a rhythm for enjoyable auto tours. After a short time in New York City, we began the six-week New England and eastern Canada research trip.

I had always wanted to go (to New England)...The beautiful spring flowers along the way to see Raymond and family in Virginia...I really did enjoy "The Music Man" (Broadway show). Guess you know that since I saw it so many times (*movie version in later years*).

At Boston, a Mr. Bigelow drove us to see historic places. Cambridge, settled in 1630, the homes of famous writers Henry W. Longfellow, Oliver Wendell Holmes and James Russell Lowell, namesake of my school in Indiana. Also saw the Paul Revere house, oldest in Boston, built about 1670 and purchased by Revere in 1770. Saw the Red School House where Mary Elizabeth Sawyer really had brought her lamb to school. John Roalston wrote the first 13 lines and Elizabeth Hale wrote the remainder of the poem "Mary's Little Lamb."

> *On picture postcard to George Strong family, May 8, 1957 (2-cent stamp postage):* Ate at restaurant in Rockport, Mass. tonight and had a good dinner. Have room and porch overlooking the bay. Is nice and cool here. The timber is so dry; we had to detour around Manchester, Mass. because of forest fire. Wasn't very far from one, and fire engines were getting hose spread out. We got out of there. Sure is scary. Will go into Maine tomorrow. Love, Mom & Jean.

Letter to family May 18, 1957, from Chateau Frontenac, Quebec:
Arrived last nite 7:10; have nice room with twin beds, chest, dresser, desk and 2 big chairs. Are way up on a hill overlooking the entire city. I never saw such hills, some long and steep. Canada is pretty country, looks like big parks all the way here. There is a big wall around Quebec City. On our walk last night after eating, we

walked downhill away from hotel and then back up. Good exercise after riding all day. *Thelma remained in New York City at the Hartig apartment on Riverside Drive (Jean's home for four years) from June 3 until June 25 when she returned home by train.*

1962 - *To Seattle World's Fair with Mark Minor and Jean.* It was an eighth grade graduation present for Mark.

1973 - *To Florida with George and family to visit Ruth Ann's at Christmas. Jean came down from Washington. Thelma stayed until January 1974 when she went by train to visit Jean in D.C.*

1957. Thelma on boardwalk at Frontenac hotel, Quebec, Canada.

52

IV
Excerpts from Thelma's Letters

August 24, 1977 letter:

"Got a letter from Joe and Ruth Ann's Monday and another letter from R.A. yesterday. Joe wrote he'd be home in a day or two but wasn't as R.A. called Saturday and he wasn't there yet. He wrote a nice letter and good writing and quite long for him. Seemed sorry he didn't make it (in Marines), but said he wants to get a job, sell his car and get a truck when he gets home."

August 29, 1977 letter:

"Was good to talk to you (Jean) yesterday. Allen seemed glad to come and eat with me. Was glad to have him, too. He had his hair cut and it looks real nice. He told me Pam has a car and then said he wasn't supposed to tell me so told him I'd be surprised when they tell me. It is red and a Dodge Dart. He said it is all paid for and Pam owes her folks $2,000 for it. Guess they got it the day before they left on vacation." . . .

"Probably will hear from Ruth Ann's today. Am anxious to know if Joe got home OK (from Marine Corps boot camp)." . . .

"Doris Mae called to see if I need eggs so will bring some Thursday. Steven likes school and is taking mechanical training so hope he makes it, and am sure he will." . . .

"Leslie will be 10 months old Sunday. Sure is growing. You should have seen my mirror after they were here Friday. She had cookie smeared over the lower 7 or 8 inches of it. Got hard and I had to rub to get it off. She loves to see herself in mirror and it keeps her out of other things."

1980. Strong family picnic, Cedar Rapids. Back from left, Darlene Strong, Eileen and Maurice Minor, Steve Neal, Joe Strickler, George Strong, Rick Neal. Front, Pam Strong, Allen Strong, Janice Strickler with second daughter, Kathy, Doris Mae with first Strickler daughter, Leslie, and Norman Neal, grandparents.

V
Remembering Our Parents

Jean Strong

My memory of our parents—Walter and Thelma Strong—is of a loving couple who, throughout 30 years of marriage, openly displayed affection for one another at home. I believe their marriage was a true and loving partnership—an ideal 20th century marriage.

Walter first became a father at age 21 (Eileen), again at 24 (me), 27 (George), 28 (Patricia Ann who did not live), 31 (Doris Mae) and at 35 (Ruth Ann). It is probable that each of us has differing memories of our father and mother because they, too, were maturing. Our dad's performance in the two weeks before Christmas convinced me, at least, that Santa was checking to see that we children were being good.

He was fleet of foot, and darkness aided the deception as he tapped on each of the five downstairs windows in our little house. I was seven or eight years old before I caught sight of him running from one window to the next where he would tap again.

Our mother was the family disciplinarian; Dad was afraid he might hurt us by spanking too hard. She enforced the good behavior message verbally, and from her (or Grandpa Strong) we learned by questioning that Santa arrived in a sleigh when snow was on the ground, by airplane—with a silent engine—when there was none. If reindeer could fly, engines could be noiseless.

Mom also taught us to speak ill of no one. "If you do not have something good to say about a person, say nothing." This opinion was also attributed to our paternal great-grandfather, Benjamin Bowman, a miller from Pennsylvania who purchased the Marion farm land in 1860 when it was referred to as "the Brody place"—so-called for the horse thieves who occupied the land in the early days. Our Grandpa G. A. Strong married Bowman's daughter, Nettie, inherited her share of the land and purchased the rest of the Marion farm. Bowman's own sons chose not to farm.

I remember spending Christmas Eve at the big house with Grandpa and Auntie. We waited in the den where Grandpa sat in his Morris chair, an oak antique that now graces my living room in Arkansas. The chair had belonged to his father. For Christmas treats, I think Auntie served popcorn and home-grown Wealthy apples from the tree in the south yard.

Excitement ran high in anticipation when Mom and Dad came to take us home to find what Santa had left under our tree. We children helped our mother decorate it after Dad strung the electric lights a week or so before Christmas Eve.

During the Depression years, there would be one big present for all of us, like a Radio Flyer wagon with removable wooden sides one year, and small individual presents. Another year, it was a toy typewriter that really worked. We always got a long cotton stocking (from our own wardrobes) stuffed with an orange, nuts and hard candy, and sometimes a small present. Milk and cookies left on the table were always gone, devoured by a hungry Santa, we assumed.

Our mother kept track of all income and major expenses. Income in 1929 was $1,722 and electricity for the little house cost $29.44 that year, she noted. Income varied during the Depression years from a low of $501 in 1932 to a high of $819 in 1935.

[An inflated 1932 and 1935 dollar is worth $15.22 in 2007.]

I remember Mom dressed chickens after Dad killed and plucked them. The family delivered them on Saturday night to customers in Cedar Rapids. Delivery was free, part of our family recreation. Mom charged twenty-five cents plus the going rate for a chicken. The customers were delighted with fresh clean fowl at modest cost—free of pin feathers outside and pristine inside.

In 1936, our last year in the little house, family income was $725. It jumped in 1937—when Dad became farm manager—to $1,754 and our electricity in the big house cost $45.20 for the year.

[1937 dollar value is $14.48 in 2007.]

Mom always kept her hands busy. When she was not cooking, cleaning, sewing, cutting someone's hair, giving a permanent, or writing letters, she was doing needlework while listening to the radio or (after 1954 when we got our first set) watching TV. The kitchen radio remained a favorite daytime companion and information source.

During radio days of the 20s, 30s, and 40s, she had favorite programs and wrote to stars like Gene and Glenn, Don McNeil (Breakfast Club) in Chicago, and Tom Breneman's Breakfast in Hollywood, California. She also wrote later to Iowa writer Meredith Willson ("Music Man"), sent birthday wishes to President Nixon— and heard from both. The farm market news was a morning program seldom missed on the farm, and Western singers, Jerry and Zelda, led into the news from Des Moines.

The family spokesperson, Mom consulted our dad in private about family matters. I learned surprising news about our father in 1944 after I told Mom I was either going to join the Waves or go to college. The next morning she told me they had talked and decided they would rather I go to college but that I should do what I most wanted to do and be.

"Your father never wanted to be a farmer," she confided. "He had a job with the railroad when he was 18 but his father needed him on the farm and told him he would disown him if he took that job. We do not want to keep any of our children from making their own choices," she said.

My mother also told me that Grandpa George Strong had the marriage of his older son, Dale, annulled because the woman had married Dale for his father's money. Uncle Dale's speech was somewhat impaired, but we children remember him as a kind and gentle man. We have a photo of Dale's son, but no information about what became of him.

In researching family history, I learned that our father's Grandmother Eliza (Mrs. Benjamin) Bowman kept a diary in which she wrote about Dale having diphtheria as a youth, and "little Walter" being thrown from his pony unhurt.

Uncle Dale worked on the family farm and lived in the big house until Grandpa died. He voluntarily accepted Earl T. Brockman as guardian of his inheritance. The money lasted until 1945, when Dale began working in the shops of the Rock Island railroad in Cedar Rapids. He died of a heart attack at age 52 in the August heat of 1949 while walking along a city street.

During Mom's lifetime, I always managed to get home for Christmas (except for a couple of holidays spent in Florida when she, too, was there). The Iowa families always congregated on Christmas Eve at her home in northeast Cedar Rapids, and Elaine Minor's birthday was celebrated as part of the dessert tradition. It was a holiday party for all the grandchildren.

Our mother never wanted to learn to drive. She was my friend and frequent travel companion in the 1950s and 60s. After I left

Cedar Rapids in 1954 and again in 1971, Ruth, Doris, and George provided transportation for her grocery and household shopping. From Geneva Tower, she walked to the beauty shop and department stores and enjoyed that independence.

During the late 40s, 50s and 60s, additional grandchildren were born. Only one great-grandchild (Leslie Strickler) arrived during Grandma's life. Nine more great-grandchildren and six great-great-grandchildren followed.

I am publishing this book so that they can know something of their Grandmother Strong who would have loved them all as much as she loved the ones she knew. She was a loving and lovable lady—with a mind of her own.

VI
Afterword

Our pharmacist friend, Lois Emanuel (who died of lung cancer in 1991) participated in the memorial service for our mother on March 15, 1978. Friends contributed three hundred dollars that we gave in Thelma's name to Camp Good Health—one of the charities for children that *The Gazette* supported and our mother favored.

The memorial service program listed her survivors: Four daughters, Mrs. Maurice (Eileen) Minor of Manchester, Iowa, Jean Strong of Washington, D.C., Mrs. Norman (Doris) Neal of Swisher, and Mrs. John (Ruth) Armstrong of Lake Worth, Florida; a son, George W. Strong of Cedar Rapids, eleven grandchildren; one great-granddaughter, and a sister, Mrs. Dora Leinen of Santa Ana, California. A daughter, Patricia, preceded her in death.

All family members, except her sister, attended the service in Marion. Thelma willed her body to science. Her ashes are buried in the family plot at Cedar Memorial Park in Cedar Rapids.

After John Armstrong's death in Florida on November 24, 2004, his widow, Ruth, moved to northwest Arkansas near her sister, Jean, who retired there in 1990.

Among the sympathy cards received by family members was one from Ella (Mrs. J. B.) Strother, a Mount Vernon farm neighbor, and the mother of Eileen's husband (Maurice Minor).

Mrs. Strother wrote:
> I always considered your Mother one of my very best friends, and shall miss her very much. Time heals our grief. Memories are with us always.

Dates of family member deaths

1914—Nettie (Mrs. George A.) Strong, mother, grandmother

1931—Samuel E. Oliver, father, grandfather

1936—George A. Strong, father, grandfather

February 23, 1944—Mary E. Oliver, mother, grandmother

June 21, 1951—Walter B. Strong, father, grandfather

May 6, 1977—Ida Strong Merkel, step-mother, "Auntie"

March 13, 1978—Thelma I. Strong, mother, grandmother

March 23, 1989—Darlene Moser Strong, daughter-in-law, aunt

June 10, 1994—George W. Strong, son, uncle

August 16, 1994—Dora Leinen, sister, aunt

August 8, 2001—Janice Neal Strickler, granddaughter, cousin

November 24, 2004—John V. Armstrong, son-in-law, uncle

January 9, 2008—Ruth A. Armstrong, daughter, grandmother

Value of $1.00 in November 2007

Selected years from 1913-2006
Based on CPI (Consumer Price Index)

Find current 2007 value of $1.00 in a prior year (birth year) and learn how inflation affects (reduces) your spendable income:

Year	Value	Year	Value	Year	Value
1913	$21.06	1945	$11.58	1981	$ 2.29
1915	$20.64	1947	$ 9.35	1982	$ 2.16
1916	$19.13	1948	$ 8.65	1983	$ 2.09
1917	$16.29	1950	$ 8.65	1984	$ 2.01
1920	$10.42	1951	$ 8.02	1986	$ 1.90
1922	$12.41	1953	$ 7.81	1987	$ 1.84
1923	$12.19	1955	$ 7.78	1990	$ 1.60
1925	$11.91	1957	$ 7.42	1995	$ 1.37
1926	$11.78	1958	$ 7.21	2000	$ 1.21
1928	$12.19	1960	$ 7.04	2005	$ 1.07
1930	$12.48	1961	$ 6.97	2006	$ 1.03
1932	$15.22	1962	$ 6.90	2007	$ 1.00
1935	$15.22	1970	$ 5.37		
1936	$15.00	1976	$ 3.66		
1937	$14.48	1977	$ 3.44		
1939	$15.00	1978	$ 3.20		
1940	$14.89	1980	$ 2.53		

Inflation Statistics Source: Bureau of Labor web site www.bls.gov

Index of Family Names

Armstrong, John
Joe, Jr.
Joe, Sr.
Ruth Ann (Mrs.)
Sue L. (Ireland)
Susie (Mrs. Joe, Sr.)

Atwater, Don
Ethel (Mrs.)
George
Harold
Isabelle (Chadim)

Bouches, Alice (Sickle)
Ray, Jr.
Raymond (Husband)

Bowman, Benjamin
Eliza (Mrs.)
Nettie

Boyson, Adolph

Braun, Christa

Brockman, Earl T.

Brown, Dr. W. E.

Burnham, Judge

Byam, Oscar
Inez (Mrs.)

Byerly, Roy
Bob
Don
Ellsworth
George
Gladys (Mrs. Roy)
Johnny
Mary (Saugstad)

Carson, Chris
Fran (Mrs.)

Craft, Art
Gladys (Mrs.)
Helen
John
Marilyn

Dant, Chris
Kimberly (Mrs.)
Natalie

Doebel, Naomi

Ebbert, Bertha

Emanuel, Lois

Epperson, John
Alpha (Mrs. John)
Lyle

Finneran, Annie
Tommie (husband)
Eileen

Finson, Roy
Dick
Dorothy (Christensen)
Zelma (Mrs. Roy)

Graham, Elmer
Ella (Mrs. Elmer)

Hartig, Morris
Jimmy (Mrs.)

Herbst, Edna

Hill, Leonard

Humke, Herman

Ireland, Edwin
Jacinda
Jamal
Sue L. (Armstrong)

Kaiser, George
Abbie
Lettie (Mrs. George)

Keith, Dr. J. J.

Kriz, Anne

Leinen, Al
Dora (Mrs.)
Eileen (Kelley)

Martin, Ray

Matteson, George
Mildred
Robert
Viola (Mrs. George)

McCammon, Ed
Blanche (Mrs.)

McMurrin, Junior (Strickler)

McVeigh, Steven
Karen (Yates)

Minor, Maurice
David
Elaine
Eileen (Mrs. Maurice)
Mark
Neoma (Mrs. Neil)
Neil

Morgan, Aunt Agnes
Mary E. (Oliver)
Uncle George

Moser, Darlene (Strong)

Neal, Norman
Doris (Mrs. Norman)
Janice (Strickler)
Karen (Yates, McVeigh)
Melissa (Mrs. Steve)
Rick
Steve

Oliver, Samuel E.
Anna "Annie" (Finneran)
Blanche (McCammon)
Clyde
Dora (Leinen)
Ethel (Peyton)
Evvie (Thoroughman)
Gladys (Byerly)
Mary E. (Mrs. Samuel)
Sherman
Thelma (Strong)

Petersen, Henry
Mae (Mrs. Henry)
Patty
Peter

Polasky, Connie

Ramsay, Miss

Schmidt, Marthella

Sickle, Alice (Bouches)

Smith, Martin (daughters)
Bernice (Felwock)
Dorothy (Mackey)
Ivadene (Bergquist)
Mae (Petersen)
Viola (Matteson)
Zelma (Finson)

Stark, Albert

Stark, Carl (carpenter)

Strickland, Marie

Strickler, Joe
Janice (Mrs. Joe)
Kathy
Leslie
Zach (McMurrin)

Strong, George
Allen R
Darlene (Mrs. George)
Pamela J.

Strong, Walter B.
Auntie (Mrs. Geo. A. 2nd, Merkel)
Dale (brother)
Darlene, (Mrs. George W.)
Doris Mae (Neal)
Eileen (Minor)
Jean
George A. (father)
George W.
Henry G. (grandfather)
Luman M. (great-grandfather)
Nettie (Bowman, Mrs. George A. 1st)
Patricia Ann (died young)
Ruth Ann (Mazgay, Armstrong)
Thelma (Mrs. Walter)

Strother, Ella (Mrs. J. B.)

Swanger, Mr. and Mrs.

Thoroughman, Ray
Evvie
Raymond, Jr.

Turner,
Heather
Holly
Pamela (Strong)

Vahl, Harold

Willson, Meredith

Yates, Jon
Amber
Duncan
Karen (Neal, Yates, McVeigh)
Kimberly (Dant)

**This page is for
Notes About Me and My Family**

Life of a Family in 20th Century Linn County

Born of loving parents in humble circumstances, Thelma Oliver Strong moved to Iowa when she was 15. She lived and worked in Cedar Rapids, and rural Marion and Mount Vernon before returning to Cedar Rapids. Her soft-spoken husband, Walter, was a farmer—not by choice—but because his father needed him on the Marion farm.

Daughter Jean says, "I hope the story we tell about the Walter Strong family—in words and pictures from the family album—inspires others to record their own legacy for succeeding generations." Jean edited, illustrated and published *Never Say Never, The Walter B. Strong Family* for the grandchildren (her nieces and nephews).

Jean recalls, "Our mother worked hard most of her life, was widowed at 51, and lived 27 more years to enjoy her expanding family, old and new friends, and our coast-to-coast travels. Letter writing and her grandchildren were her passions."

A University of Iowa graduate, Jean Strong previously published three books since retiring in 1986 from Time-Life Books. They are *A Prairie Almanac, 1839-1919* about Linn County pioneer life, a 100-year history of Marion and its library, and a book of newspaper columns about northwest Arkansas where she currently lives.

Printed in the United States
103173LV00004B/397-453/P